The Surprise Box

by Francis Robin

Illustrated by Toni Goffe

PEARSON

Glenview, Illinois • Boston, Massachusetts • Chandler, Arizona
Upper Saddle River, New Jersey

Rosa is Martita's big sister.
Rosa gives Martita a special box.

Rosa gives Martita a wing.
Martita puts it in the box.

Rosa gives Martita a ribbon.
Martita puts it in the box.

star

Her teacher gives Martita a star.
Martita puts it in the box.

box

star

ribbon

wing

Martita loves her special things.
She loves her big sister too.

"Surprise!" says Martita.
Martita gives the box to her sister.
"Thank you!" says Rosa.

Rosa opens the box.
The box is special.
"You are special," says Rosa.